FALL OF THE GOLDEN AGE

By Alyce McPherson

FALL OF THE GOLDEN AGE

By Alyce McPherson

Empyrion Press
PO Box 140914
Broken Arrow OK 74014
918-277-3459
university@rickmanis.com

Fall of the Golden Age
Copyright © 2010 by Alyce McPherson

ISBN: 9781453642375

Empyrion Press
PO Box 140914
Broken Arrow OK 74014
918-277-3458
university@rickmanis.com

Unless otherwise noted, all Scripture quotations are from the King James Version of the Bible.

Bold type is added by the author for emphasis.

Printed in the United States of America

DEDICATION

This book is dedicated to the late Irene Lindsey, who was instrumental in stirring up the Spirit of Revelation in Me.

Contents

Introduction

In a beginning, there was a **golden age,** a time when man lived and did not die. A time when man walked with God in such close communion that death had no recognition or power. **Innocence of evil,** protected the first man Adam, but also became a snare to him when faced with a **knowledge** that appealed to the **lust of the flesh, the lust of the eyes, and a knowledge desired to make him wise.**

1 John 2:16: For all that is in the world, the lust of the flesh, the lust of the eyes, and the pride of life, is not of the father, but of the world.

Chapter 1

CREATION

Genesis 1:1: In the beginning God created the heaven and the earth. And the earth was without form and void, and darkness was upon the face of the deep. And the Spirit of God moved upon the face of the waters, and God said, **"Let there be light,"** and there was light.

If we take the above scripture at face value, **what was the light** mentioned in verse one? The sun, moon and stars were not created until the fourth day!

We must realize that the first chapter of Genesis is God's plan and purpose for man hidden in symbolism. Symbolism, according to Webster's dictionary means: Something that stands for or represents another thing. When we see the word **dove,** we think of **peace.** The **cross** represents **Christianity,** and a **lamb** is immediately identified with **Jesus,** who was the **Lamb of God,** that took away the sin of the world through His death, burial and resurrection.

The scripture declares the word of God as being light:

Psalm 119:105 (KJV): Thy word is a lamp unto my feet, and a light unto my path.

Jesus, as the word made flesh declared:

John 8:12 (KJV): Then spake Jesus again unto them, saying, I am the light of the world: he that followeth me shall not walk in darkness, but shall have the light of life.

John 1:4-5 (KJV): In him was life; and the life was the light of men. [5] And the light shineth in darkness; and the darkness comprehended it not.

John 12:46 (KJV): I am come a light into the world, that

whosoever believeth on me should not abide in darkness.

2 Cor. 4:6 (KJV): For God, who commanded the light to shine out of darkness, hath shined in our hearts, to give the light of the knowledge of the glory of God in the face of Jesus Christ.

The **light was God's divine intention to bring both heaven and earth out of darkness and gather His creation into oneness with Himself.**

Ephesians 1:9,10: Having made known unto us the mystery of His will, according to His good pleasure which He hath purposed in Himself, that in the dispensation of the fullness of times, He might **gather together in one, all things in Christ, both which are in heaven and which are on earth, even in Him.**

The above scripture tells us that God **purposed in Himself!** God is omnipotent, all power, all dominion, authority and wisdom.

God is the great creator of all things, visible and invisible and anyone who desires to create something, does not haphazardly begin his creation without an idea of what he wants to create. The first step is to have the finished product in mind, plus a plan in how to begin and finally what steps are to be taken to bring the visionary image into visible reality.

If God's intention was to **gather all things into Christ,** then He must first of all **create all things.**

There has been continual dispute between the **theory of creation and the theory of evolution.** Religion insists that Adam was created in a twenty-four hour day six thousand years ago. Science however, declares that man evolved from the ape and has walked the earth for millions of years. Religion declares that the Bible is the infallible word of God, and science refuses to accept this theory and has shown proof that man existed millions of years before Adam. Which theory are we to believe? As children of faith in the word of God, do we dogmatically shut our ears and our eyes to infallible proof revealed by the scientific community, or do we open our hearts and minds and realize that in the economy of God science and religion agree!

2 Pet. 3:5: Amplified translation: For they willfully overlook and forget this (fact), that heavens (came into) existence long ago by the word of God, and an earth also which was formed

out of water, and by means of water, through which the world
that then (existed) was deluged with water and perished.

The above scripture tells us in no uncertain terms that all things came into existence long ago by the word of God, and that same word **formed an earth out of water and by means of water.** This scripture would certainly support the theory of evolution! Let's gird up the loins of our mind here and see what actually happened.

Man indeed evolved out of water. If all the water in our physical body was removed, there would only be left the ashes of a few minerals. We are formed in the womb of our mother safe and protected inside a sac of water. It is only at the point of birth that our journey in water ends and we find ourselves breathing oxygen and walking on terra firma.

All plant and animal life evolved over millions of years, and the pre-Adam man who evolved, developed in stages, until he was able to function in human fashion. **This man did not evolve from an ape, or a fish, but was a SPECIE unto himself.** He was capable of hunting, tool making and had the mental capacity to worship all creature comforts that support life.

It was **from this specie,** that God **formed the first man Adam!**

Proverbs 8:23: I was set up from everlasting, from the beginning, or ever the earth was. When there were no depths, I was brought forth, before the mountains were settled, before the hills was I brought forth; while as yet He had not made the earth, nor the fields, nor the HIGHEST PART OF THE DUST OF THE WORLD.

The above scripture reveals wisdom speaking, but the phrase **highest part of the dust of the world,** has a significant meaning:

The pre-Adam man was the **highest part, the chief** and the most **excellent,** of all God's creation. His capacity of intelligence far surpassed all the animal kingdom, and it was this man that was chosen to be the beginning, the captain and the ruler over all the earth.

THE WORLD:

Hebrew 8398 Strong's: *Tobel,* from Hebrew 2986 (yabal); the earth (as moist and therefore inhabited); by extensive the globe; by implication its inhabitants; specifically a participle land.

The word for world in the above scripture represents not only the terra-firma, but can also include the **inhabitants** that dwell there, or the **orderly arrangement of things.**

Chapter 2

CREATION OF
ADAM

Gen. 1:1: In the beginning God created the heaven and the earth. And the earth was without form and void, and darkness was upon the face of the deep. And the Spirit of God moved upon the face of the waters. And God said, "Let there be light," and there was light.

Let's examine two words in the above scripture:

FORM:

Hebrew 8414, Strong's: *Tohuw*, from an unused root meaning to lie waste; a desolation (of surface), desert; figurative a worthless thing; adverbial in vain, confusion, empty place, without form, nothing, vain, waste, wilderness.

VOID:

Hebrew 922, Strong's: *Bohuw* from an unused root (meaning to be empty): a vacuity, (superficially) and undistinguishable ruin, emptiness, void.

We see that the Hebrew words **without form and void** means, **confused and empty.**

This was the condition of the pre-Adam man that roamed the earth six-thousand years ago. Although he was the **highest part of the dust** of God's creation, he was confused and empty for darkness was upon the face or direction of his deep. He had no knowledge or relationship with his creator, God.

Gen. 1:26: And God said, let us make man in our image, after our likeness; and let them have dominion over the fish of the sea and over the fowl of the air, and over the cattle, and over all the earth, and over every creeping thing that creepeth upon the earth.

Let's examine the word **MAKE.**

Hebrew 6213, Strong's: *Asah,* a primitive root; to do or make, in the broadest sense and widest application (as follows) accomplish, **advance,** appoint, apt, be at, become, bear, bestow, bring forth, bruise, be busy, etc.

The word **make,** means to **ADVANCE!** Remember that God had sworn by Himself that in the dispensation of the fullness of times He would gather all things into Christ; the pre-Adam man was chosen to **BE ADVANCED INTO GOD'S LIKENESS AND IMAGE!**

Gen. 2:7: And the Lord God formed man of the dust of the ground, and breathed into his nostrils the breath of life and man became a living soul.

The word FORMED in the Hebrew has the following meaning:

Hebrew 3335, Strong's: *Yatsar*, probably identical with Hebrew 3334 (yatsar) (through the squeezing into shape);

God moved upon the pre-Adam man and breathed His quickening Spirit of life into him. This life of God gave man the **capacity to communicate** with his creator. Man became a **living soul!** He was given eternal life and became body, soul and spirit! He became the **FIRST MAN ADAM,** not the **FIRST MAN,** but the **FIRST MAN ADAM!**

The **I AM** gave the first man Adam dominion over the world, or orderly arrangement of things, because Adam was the light or divine intention of God that shone in the dispensation of the **golden age. Adam was Gods representative figure in the earth. He became the ruling authority of the day.**

The word **NAME** has a significant meaning in the scripture. A person's name was not merely a title, but was given to describe a person's **character or nature.**

There are several places in the Bible, where God Himself changed people's names **according to the calling** He had placed upon their lives.

The name Jacob carries the meaning of usurper. He was

given this name or nature by his parents because he stole the birthright and blessing from his elder brother Esau through deceit and cunning. When he prevailed with God however, God gave him the name Israel, meaning, he will rule as God.

The parents of Abraham gave him the name Abram, meaning **high father,** but God changed his name to **Abraham, father of a multitude.**

St. John 14:13,14: And whatsoever ye shall ask in my name, that will I do, that the Father may be glorified in the Son. If ye shall ask any thing in my name, I will do it.

Only when man knows the name or nature of God can they call upon Him, have dealings with Him or bring Him into play.

When the name or nature is pronounced, the one invoked appears or works, for the pronouncement of the name sets in operation the **potential energy or nature,** within the name.

By giving someone a name, one establishes a relationship of dominion and possession toward him. When God breathed His Spirit into the man, God possessed him and established a relationship described through the **name AD-AM. The nature of Ad-Am described the nature of one who is an Addition to the I AM.**

*God did not **name** the rest of His creation; Adam did:*

*Genesis 2:19: And out of the ground the Lord God formed every beast of the field, and every fowl of the air, and brought them unto Adam to see what he would call them; and whatsoever Adam **called every living creature, that was the name thereof.***

Verse 20: And Adam gave names to all cattle, and to the fowl of the air and to every beast of the field; but for Adam there was not found a help meet for him.

The word **help meet** has the following meaning:

Hebrew 5826, Strong's: *Azar*, a primitive root; to surround, protect or aid; help, succour

Adam needed a **counterpart, an equal, on the same spiritual plane as himself.** Adam was formed from the **higher part** of the dust of the earth! He had become a **living soul;** a specie that had become an extension of God Himself in the earth.

Notice how the following scripture reads:

Genesis 2:18: And the Lord God said, It is not good that the man should be alone; I will make him an help meet for him.

I will make **him a help MEET for him.** Notice the phrase is, help **meet** not help **mate.** It was God's intention to make a counterpart, an equal, one who could communicate with the man on the level of his understanding.

Genesis 2:19-20 (KJV): And out of the ground the Lord God formed every beast of the field, and every fowl of the air; and brought them unto Adam to see what he would call them: and whatsoever Adam called every living creature, that was the name thereof. [20] And Adam gave names to all cattle, and to the fowl of the air, and to every beast of the field; ***but for Adam there was not found an help meet for him.***

Genesis 2:21,25: And the Lord God caused a deep sleep to fall upon Adam and he slept; and he took ***one of his ribs****, and closed up the flesh instead thereof; and the rib, which the Lord God had taken from man, made he a woman, and brought her unto the man. And Adam said this is now bone of my bones and* *flesh of my flesh; she shall be called woman, because she was taken out of man.*

Therefore shall a man leave his father and his mother, and shall cleave unto his wife; and they shall be one flesh. And they were both naked, the man and his wife and were not ashamed.

The **rib** referred to in the above scripture means **chamber.**

The Hebrew word translated **rib** in both the Authorized and Revised versions of the Bible occurs forty-two times in the Old Testament, but it is in this scripture alone translated **rib.**

In the majority of cases it is translated **side or sides** and in other places corners or chambers, but never rib or ribs except in these two verses describing the separation of the woman from the man, Adam.

In the Septuagint version of scripture, the word is **pleura,** which Homer, Hesiod and Herodotus used for **side, not rib.**

The rib taken from Adam represents chamber. The woman was taken from the very **soul** of the first man Adam.

She represented the **total fulfillment** of his **desire and need.** Only out of Adam could the woman be found.

The woman was the feminine **side,** and the **equal counter part of Adam's soul,** she was taken from the **seat of his affections and became woman or WOMB MAN OF CREATION.**

When Jesus died on the cross as the last man Adam, out of His **pierced side, out of His chamber, out of His soul, a rib was taken, and the early church was born; the BRIDE OF CHRIST!**

Isa. 53:12: Therefore will I divide him a portion with the great, and he shall divide the spoil with the strong; because he hath POURED OUT HIS SOUL; unto death,

When Jesus Christ walked in the days of His flesh, He communicated unto the twelve Apostles the true nature of who He was. Out of the very innermost recesses of His **soul** came the word or seed that would be conceived by the woman being formed from His very own substance.

The Apostle Paul tells us in:

Ephesians 5:30: For we are members of his body, of his flesh, and of his bones;

When He went away the twelve Apostles instituted the early church built upon the foundation of all that Jesus had taught them. All our faith is founded upon the word that came from the lips of Jesus Christ, His death, burial and resurrection.

The church is the **womb man** of Jesus Christ: She is set forth to be the mother of all living in the realm of spirit. **JERUSALEM FROM ABOVE! THE MOTHER OF US ALL!**

All creation is groaning and travailing, waiting for the church to produce the offspring of Christ!

*Romans 8:19: For the earnest expectation of the creature waited for the **manifestation of the sons of God.***

Chapter 3

ADAM'S DOMINION

In the **golden age of Adam,** was a dispensation of innocence. Adam had no **intimate or experiential** knowledge of sin and death. Life and longevity ruled in Adam's domain. Man lived for hundreds of years, in response to the **unchallenged** spirit of life manifest in the earth.

Man began to cultivate the earth and reaped a bountiful harvest. The earth yielded its strength to man as all creation walked in the **innocence of sin and death.**

Temple worship began, and Adam became the first **Melchizedek priest.**

The Apostle Paul speaks of Melchizedek in the following scripture:

Hebrews 7:1,28: For this Melchizedek king of Salem, priest of the most high God, who met Abraham returning from the slaughter of the kings, and blessed him; To whom also Abraham gave a tenth part of all; first being by interpretation King of righteousness, and after that also King of Salem, which is, King of peace; Without father, without mother, without descent, having neither beginning of days, nor end of life; but make like unto the Son of God; abideth a priest continually.

Melchizedek was without father, without mother, without descent, having neither beginning of days, nor end of life; but made like unto the Son of God.

If you will read the rest of the chapter you will see that Paul is comparing the priesthood of Melchizedek with the

Levitical priesthood instituted under the law of Moses.

The priesthood of Aaron sprang out of only one of the twelve tribes of Israel, the tribe of Levi. Aaron was the first, and all succeeding high priests would come from his lineage. When each high priest died, the office would automatically pass to the eldest son.

The priesthood of Melchizedek however, was after the order of an endless life. It was not continued from natural descent, it had no beginning for it was birthed from the loins of eternal God. It had no end, for Jesus restored this everlasting priesthood and abides forever as our great high priest. He lives evermore to make intercession for us!

Psalm 110:4: The Lord hath sworn, and will not repent, thou art a priest for ever after the order of Melchizedek.

The following is taken from Matthew Henry's Commentary of the Bible:

Christ is God's Minister to us, and our Advocate with the Father, and so is the Mediator between God and man. He is a Priest of the order of Melchizedek, which was before that of Aaron, and on many accounts superior to it, and a more

lively representation of it.

The priesthood of Melchizedek, ruled in the days of Adam with a **rod of authority that subdued all other religious orders of that day.**

The benefit of its power was experienced by all who lived under the dominion of its rule. All creation enjoyed the spiritual atmosphere that accompanied the presence of this powerful priesthood.

The priesthood of Melchizedek traveled to all the known world at that time. We find traces of its roots in all the nations of the world. Almost all eastern nations have a creation story similar to the account found in the book of Genesis. The explanation of creation is basically the same; with the exception the cast of characters have different names.

When Columbus discovered America he found the native Indian worshiping the God as revealed to them by the **great white gods** that appeared on their shores centuries before!

Genesis 2:10: And a river went out of Eden to water the garden; and from thence it was parted, and became into four heads.

The river mentioned above is the **pure word of life,** ministered by Adam, as he dressed and kept the garden of God.

After the fall, however, the river of truth became infiltrated with humanistic teaching and as a result parted and became **four heads or four great religious orders.** The teachings of Melchizedek is represented by the river **Euphrates,** and the other three rivers, Pison, Gihon and Hiddekel evolved into Hinduism, Islam and Baalism, the **seat of Eastern Philosophy.**

When the sons of God, or the **Melchizedek priests** began to marry the **daughters of men (other religious factions whose worship was based in humanism),** the order of an endless life became infiltrated with humanistic teachings that created **religious giants** in the earth. They were giants in regard to earthy creation's observance. Remember when the children of Israel desired a king, God gave them Saul, who stood **head and shoulders above every man?**

In the book of Revelation, the apostle John saw **four angels or messengers bound in the great river Euphrates, loosed!**

When God gave the **LAW** to Moses on Mount Sinai, all other religious beliefs were **bound.** These religions were not destroyed, but bound in the sense that **God was moving within the confines of the law.** There was no spiritual blessing on any other mode of worship. The Melchizedek priesthood had been consumed through four hundred years of captivity in Egypt, and remained only a vague memory in the minds and history of the Hebrew people. The people who came from beyond the flood!

We see then that the Melchizedek Priesthood in it's **fallen state** is represented by the **law** and became known as the Levitical Priesthood. As long as creation remained under the confines of the law, **eastern philosophy was bound!**

When Jesus **fulfilled the law,** He ushered in the dispensation of **grace.** Grace is unmerited favor bestowed upon man! Grace rains spiritual blessing upon the just and unjust alike. We have been under the outpouring of Grace now for two thousand years and the result has been the **release of the four messengers bound in Euphrates or bound by the law of Moses!**

Rev. 9:13: And the sixth angel sounded, and I heard a voice from the horns of the golden altar which is before God, saying to the sixth angel, which had the trumpet, LOOSE THE FOUR ANGELS, which are BOUND in the great RIVER EUPHRATES.

When the law was fulfilled, Euphrates became **Christianity,** and the other three angels or messengers loosed under grace were, **Hinduism, Baalism, and Islam , EASTERN PHILOSOPHY!**

We see Eastern Philosophy today in the **New Age Movement.** It is the great counterfeit of truth. It is based upon humanism and exalts man's carnality. There is enough truth contained within its teachings, that it has the power to deceive the very elect of God, unless we have the word of God written upon the tables of our hearts.

When Jesus overcame death, hell and the grave an eternal priesthood was instituted after the order of Melchizedek. Jesus became the high priest of our profession and rules after the order of an endless life.

Hebrews 3:1: Wherefore, holy brethren, partakers of the heavenly calling, consider the Apostle and High Priest of our profession, Christ Jesus.

Hebrews 4:14,15: Seeing then that we have a great high priest, that is passed into the heavens, Jesus the Son of God, let us hold fast our profession.

Jesus instituted a new priesthood after the order of an endless life. He abides a High Priest continually and is seated at the right hand of authority, high above every principality and power!

Hebrews 6:20: Whither the forerunner is for us entered, even Jesus, made an high priest for ever after the order of Melchizedek.

We see then that Jesus restored the divine order of Melchizedek and the river Euphrates has become a pure river of life that is once again dressing and keeping the garden of God in the earth.

Rev. 22:1,6: And he shewed me a pure river of water of life, clear as crystal, proceeding out of the throne of God and of the Lamb. In the midst of the street of it, and on either side of the river, was there the tree of life.

What a restoration! What a life! He is alive forevermore. All other moves in the earth will once again become **one river,** one truth that will be life to all creation.

Habakkuk 2:14: For the earth shall be filled with the knowledge of the glory of the Lord, as the waters cover the sea.

Chapter 4

THE FALL

Genesis 3:1: Now the serpent was more subtle than any beast of the field which the Lord God had made. And he said unto the woman, yea hath God said, ye shall not eat of every tree of the garden?

First of all let's deal with the SERPENT!

In the days of Adam there were many religious orders referred to as the **beasts of the field.** The serpent mentioned in this scripture represents one of these orders that was **more subtle** than any of the other orders of that day.

In ancient Babylon where Adam and Eve lived, there was in the city of **Der,** a religious cult called **Sachan.** This cultic order worshiped a **serpent deity.**[1]

The serpent that came to Eve was not a natural snake, but was the **doctrine of Sachan.**

Notice that the tree mentioned in Gen 3:1, was the tree of the **knowledge of good and evil.**

Tree in the Hebrew means:

Hebrew 6086, Strong's: *Ets*, from Hebrew 6095, a tree (from its firmness);

The tree of the knowledge of good and evil was a **firmly established knowledge in the midst of the garden.**

Genesis 2:9: And out of the ground made the Lord God to grow every tree that is pleasant to the sight, and good for food; the tree of life also in the midst of the garden, and the tree of

---

[1] Kittles Theological Dictionary of the New Testament

knowledge of good and evil.

Let's examine the word midst:

Hebrew 8432, Strong's: *Tavek,* from an unused root meaning to sever; a bi-section, by implication the centre.

Within the very **midst** of Adam, was a **vanity** or weakness subject to those things that satisfied the earthy nature of his beginning (Romans chapter 8).

The knowledge presented to him by the serpent appealed to the lust of his flesh, the lust of his eye and a knowledge desired to make him as God.

God had given Adam warning that if he ingested this knowledge he would die.

Genesis 2:16,17: And the Lord God commanded the man saying; of every tree of the garden thou mayest freely eat, but of the tree of the knowledge of good and evil, thou shalt not eat of it; for in the day that thou eatest thereof thou shalt surely die.

The serpent did not tempt Adam, but went to the woman or, the **WOMB MAN of Adam!**

*Genesis 3:1,3: Now the serpent was more subtle than any beast of the field which the Lord God had made, and he said unto the woman, yea hath God said, ye shall not eat of every tree of the garden? And the woman said unto the serpent, we may eat of the fruit of the trees of the garden; but of the fruit of the tree which is in the **midst** of the garden, God hath said, ye shall not eat of it, neither shall ye touch it lest ye die.*

And the serpent said unto the woman, ye shall not surely die; for God doth know that in the day ye eat thereof, then your eyes shall be opened, and ye shall be as gods, knowing good and evil.

Notice that in the above scripture there are two words that are very significant in understanding the nature of the fall of man.

First of remember the word **midst** means; to sever; a bisection, centre. Within the very **center or midst** of man are two trees, or **two firmly established natures!**

One tree within the midst of man has its roots grounded in the **base nature of his earthy humanity.** Its branches produce fruit after the earthy image from whence Adam was taken.

The second tree located in the midst of man is the tree of life. Its roots are found within the **divine life** breathed into Adam in his formation.

If you will notice the word **midst** also means **bi-section**! Both trees are found in the garden of Adam's being yet there is a division or bi-section that separates the two trees or firmly established truths!

The other word **touch** means: To lay the hand upon.

A heightened definition for the word touch means not merely to touch an object, but to touch it all around and through. I can touch a piano, but one who has mastered the instrument can touch it in such a way as to know it in it's entirety or **experientially.**

God had given the man and woman a warning, and told them the results of touching and ingesting the humanistic teachings prevalent in their natural habitat. They were to live separate lives in constant communication with spirit.

The tree of the knowledge of good and evil was very appealing to the woman. It was good for food, (it appealed to the lust of the flesh), it was pleasant to the eyes (it appealed to her intellectual and emotional desire), and it was a knowledge desired to make one wise. (It appealed to her spirit).

*Genesis 3:6: And when the woman **saw** that the tree was good for food, and that it was pleasant to the eyes, and a tree desired to make one wise, she took of the fruit thereof and did eat, and gave also unto her husband with her; and he did eat.*

*Verse 7: And the **eyes of them both were opened!***

Does this mean that Adam and his wife had walked around all this time with their eyes shut? Of course not! The word for eye in the Hebrew means:

Hebrew 5869, Strong's: *Ayin*, a fountain (as the eye of the landscape):

Adam and his wife had a **revelation.** They saw before them in the future the **fulfilled plan of God!** They saw the Lord Jesus Christ as the **last man Adam,** crucified, buried and standing up again in resurrection power and dominion. They saw themselves as earthy mediums, God's earthy garden out of which He would produce an **only begotten son.** They saw their **earthy lineage die** on the cross, and saw themselves **subject to vanity.**

*(Quote): Whether we are controlled by good or evil powers depend upon our **Spiritual vision or values.** We can only **evaluate** what we have **vision to see.** If our **sense of higher values** has not been awakened, we only **function in a lower base realm.** Higher values **must be discovered** before they can be appreciated. (End Quote).*[2]

When Adam and Eve's eyes were opened to the forward view of God's purpose for man, they evaluated what they saw and chose to walk away from the presence (or forward view) of the Lord.

St. John 1:14: And the Word was made flesh, and dwelt among us, (and we beheld his glory, the glory as of the only begotten of the Father), full of grace and truth.

The word begotten means only-born, sole, only begotten child; He who has the issue of the Father in His loins. Jesus was both son of man and son of God. Isaiah the prophet declared:

Isaiah 53:8: He was taken from prison and from judgment; and who shall declare his generation? For he was cut off out of the

---

[2] Mildred Eslik Garner

land of the living, for the transgression of my people was he stricken.

Acts 8:33: In his humiliation his judgment was taken away; and who shall declare his generation? For his life is taken from the earth.

Jesus as the last man Adam, was cut off from the land of the living, leaving no offspring in the earth.

When He arose as the **firstborn of a new creation,** He became the **only begotten Son of God!** He was not born from an earthy lineage, but was produced by the Spirit. He had the issue or seed line of the eternal Father in His loins! This is what Adam saw; an end of his earthy identity and became **naked or unclothed in his own sight.**

Genesis 3:8: And they heard the voice of the Lord God walking in the garden in the cool of the day; and Adam and his wife hid themselves from the presence of the Lord God amongst the trees of the garden.

They heard the voice of the Lord God walking in the **cool of the day.**

The following definition is given by the Strong's for the word cool:

Hebrew 7307, Strong's: *Ruwach*, from Hebrew 7306, wind, by resemblance, breath, a sensible or even violent exhalation, figurative life, anger, **insubstantiality;** by extensive a region of the sky; by resemblance **spirit but only of a rational being (including it's expression and functions).**

Adam and Eve began to walk in **insubstantiality, rationally minded in their expression and function!**

In their condemnation, they tried to hide from the **presence of the Lord.** The Hebrew word for presence used here is **face .**

The face of God reveals the **direction or purpose of God, the forward view.** Adam and his wife were trying to hide from the plan of God by hiding among the **trees or doctrinal teaching surrounding them.**

Genesis 3:9: And the Lord God called unto Adam, and said unto him, where art thou?

Verses 10/11: And he said I heard thy voice in the garden and I was afraid, and because I was naked; and I hid myself, And he said, Who told thee that thou wast naked? Hast thou eaten of the tree, whereof I commanded thee that thou shouldest not eat?

Who told thee thou wast naked?

Adam saw himself naked. We see the first example of condemnation in this scripture. Condemnation will take all who walk in it's judgment to the grave.

St. John 3:19: And this is the condemnation, that light is come into the world, and men loved darkness rather than light, because their deeds were evil.

Light will always bring condemnation to the flesh. Self preservation is the basic instinct of the animal kingdom. Man in his humanity is beast like in nature and will always seek to save himself from destruction. When Jesus was twelve years of age and at the temple at Jerusalem, He declared God to be His father.

Yet when He was baptized of John in the river Jordan, and heard God declare Him to be His son, the **spirit drove Him** into he wilderness to be tempted of the Devil. He was driven because of what He had heard the Father speak into His spirit. Jesus had a revelation by the spirit and this revelation began to drive Him from the **presence or forward view of what had been spoken in spirit.**

He was tried in every realm of His being body, soul and spirit, on the word, "This is my beloved Son in whom I am well pleased."

After fasting forty days and nights He was very hungry and began to see the stones around Him as bread. He reasoned within Himself, **If,** I am indeed the Son of God, I can turn those stones into bread." Realizing the temptation of Satan, He then replied, "Man shall not live by bread alone, but by every word that proceeded out of the mouth of God."

When Satan took Him to the pinnacle of the temple in Jerusalem, Jesus was tempted to cast Himself down.

St. Matthew 4:6: And saith unto Him, if thou be the Son of God, cast thyself down for it is written, He shall give his angels charge concerning thee and in their hands they shall bear thee up, lest at any time thou dash thy foot against a stone.

Jesus knew the scripture, and was tempted to leap off the temple to prove He was the Son of God. He knew if He was who God had declared Him to be, that divine intervention would be His for God would preserve Him for the cross. His declaration was, "Thou shalt not tempt the Lord thy God."

St. Matthew 4:8,9: Again, the devil taketh him up into an exceeding high mountain, and sheweth him all the kingdoms of the world, and the glory of them, and saith unto him, all these things will I give thee, if thou wilt fall down and worship me.

Jesus' answer was, "Get thee hence Satan, for it is written, thou shalt worship the Lord thy God, and Him only shalt thou serve."

We are always tried for the word's sake, because of the serpent's seed that is constantly trying to survive in mankind.

Job was a perfect and upright man in his generation, but came under accusation by Satan. He constantly maintained his integrity while his comforters tried to convince him he had sinned.

When Job **saw God,** he repented and became abased before his creator.

Job 42:5: I have heard of thee by the hearing of the ear, but now mine eye seeth thee.

The law of Moses was light to the nation of Israel, but was also condemnation to their flesh. It was a constant condemnation and reminder of their sinful nature and is referred to by the Apostle Paul as the **law of sin and death.**

Revelation must be received by faith and the faithful must walk in faith!

Galatians 3:11: But that no man is justified by the law in the sight of God, it is evident; for, the just shall live by faith.

Condemnation has been the influential power of death now for six thousand years! Condemnation comes when our eyes are opened into the realm of Spirit and we see the **glory of God's forward view.** It is only through faith in the death, burial and resurrection of our kinsman redeemer, that we can behold the face of God and live.

Romans 8:1: There is therefore now no condemnation to them which are in Christ Jesus, who walk not after the flesh, but after the Spirit.

When a governmental power wants to acquire property, the law declares that the property can be condemned and possessed.

Paul was telling us in the above scripture that we were purchased and redeemed by the Lord Jesus Christ and now belong to Him. We can no longer be condemned or repossessed by the powers of sin and death! We are born free and are alive forevermore in Him.

We can look into an open heaven and see the revealed will of God to man, and not be ashamed or condemned.

Our old man is dead, buried and resurrected in Jesus Christ and has passed from death to life.

As He is, so are we in this world.

1 John 4:1: Herein is our love made perfect, that we may have boldness in the day of judgment; because as He is, so are we in this world.

Chapter 5

JUDGMENTS

Genesis 3:14: And the Lord God said unto the serpent, because thou hast done this thou art cursed above all cattle, and above every beast of the field; upon thy belly shalt thou go, and dust shalt thou eat all the days of thy life.

Upon thy **BELLY** shalt thou go!

The Hebrew word for belly is taken from two words:

Hebrew 1512, Strong's: *Gachown*, the external abdomen, belly (as the source of the fetus).

Hebrew 1518: *glyach*, a primitive root; to gush forth (as water) generally to issue.

We see then that the judgment passed upon the serpent was that he would survive only as long as he could **project his seed from generation to generation as a birth within man.**

The **womb of mankind is the mind.** It is the fertile ground into which all seed must fall.

All life has its beginning in **Word.** The word is seed and will reproduce itself.

St John 1:1,3: In the beginning was the word, and the word was with God, and the word was God. All things were made by him; and without him was not any thing made that was made.

Verse 14: And the Word was made flesh, and dwelt among us, (and we beheld his glory, the glory as of he only begotten of the Father), full of grace and truth.

The **Word was in God,** for God and the Word are one and the same. God is Spirit, and the Word is the divine expression of Spirit.

Judgments

When the angel appeared to Mary, a word was spoken into her consciousness. The scripture tells us that she pondered this word in her heart or mind, and the Word became flesh and manifested itself through Jesus. He was birthed from Word and became the visible manifestation of the nature contained within that seed.

When the word or seed of the serpent was sown into the mind of the woman or womb man and was conceived as a mixture of good and evil. It was manifest as Cain and Abel.

Within the midst of each and every one of us, there is the mixture of the knowledge of good and evil. This mixture is seed sown six thousand years ago in the days of Adam.

The seed of the serpent has steadily produced Cain and Abel, and we see earthy Cain, constantly seeking to kill righteous Abel so that he might live on in generations to come.

The serpent's seed has been surviving off our dust and will continue to do so until the manifestation of the sons of God.

Romans 8:3: For what the law could not do, in that it was weak through the flesh, God sending His own Son in the likeness of sinful flesh, and for sin, condemned sin in the flesh.

Romans 8:15: For ye have not received the spirit of bondage again to fear; but ye have received the Spirit of adoption, whereby we cry, Abba, Father.

We have received the Spirit of adoption. Religion has taught us that we are children of God by adoption, but the truth of the matter is, we are children of God by birth. We are born again of the very substance of God, **Word and Spirit.**

The Hebrews had a custom in the day this scripture was written. When a child was born into a family, he was not named until he was eight days old.

The child was then placed under governors and tutors until he reached the age of thirty years. The father would then perform an **adoption ceremony,** and place his ring of authority upon the hand of his son. This ring gave the son power to execute the father's will, and gave him authority to conduct business in the father's name.

Romans 8:18, 19: For I reckon that the sufferings of this present time are not worthy to be compared with the glory, which shall be revealed in us. For the earnest expectation of the creature waited for the manifestation of the sons of God.

The word manifestation means:

Greek, 602, Strong's: *Apocalypses*, meaning disclosure, appearing, coming, lighten, manifestation, be revealed, revelation.

It is taken from a root word meaning:

Greek 602, Strong's: *Apokalupto*, to take off the cover, disclose, reveal.

All creation is groaning and travailing for a divine disclosure, where God removes a covering and reveals the sons of God. The sign or **witness of this event is the REDEMPTION OF OUR BODY!**

Romans 8:23: And not only they, but ourselves also, which have the first fruits of the Spirit, even we ourselves groan within ourselves, waiting for the adoption, to wit, the redemption of our body.

Genesis 3:18: And I will put enmity between thee and the woman, and between thy seed and her seed; it shall BRUISE THY HEAD, and thou shalt BRUISE HIS HEEL.

God told the serpent that there would be continual warfare between his seed and the seed of the woman. The result of this enmity would be the BRUISING of the serpents head, and the BRUISING of the heel of the woman's seed.

This was a prophecy concerning a time when Jesus Christ, the seed of a woman, would destroy the dominion or headship of the serpent.

The prophecy declared the heel of the woman's seed would be bruised. The following is a definition of the word heel:

Hebrew 6119, Strong's: *Aqeh*, a heel (as protuberant); hence a track; figurative the rear of an army, a lier in wait.

When Jesus Christ as the seed of the woman died on the cross, the head of the serpent was bruised. The serpent lost it's dominion in man through the sinless life of the woman's seed. There was found no trace of mixture in Jesus. He was the last man Adam, the culmination of God's formative process begun four thousand years ago when God breathed the breath of life into the **figure of him that was to come, Adam.**

Romans 5:14: Nevertheless death reigned from Adam to

Moses, even over them that had not sinned after the similitude of Adam's transgression, who is the figure of him that was to come.

The seed of the woman was affected by the bruising or overwhelming of the heel.

Jesus rendered the serpent's seed inactive within Himself, but we are still aware of the track of the serpent in our humanity.

If you will notice the word heel also means rear of an army. The early church was the forefront of God's great army in the earth. Down through the centuries of time, the battle has been raging between God's army in the earth, and the seed of the serpent. We who are alive today are beginning to realize that we are the people upon whom the end of the age has come. We are the rear guard and there is a liar in wait seeking to overwhelm us in subtlety and deception.

We are facing the same serpent today that deceived man in the golden age. The mixture of good and evil is being presented today through eastern philosophy. This message preys upon the desires of our humanity. Jesus declared however, "I am the way, the truth and the life." He has won the battle. He has prevailed and overwhelmed the dominion of the serpent's seed.

Genesis 3:17: And unto Adam he said, because thou hast hearkened unto the voice of thy wife, and hast eaten of the tree of which I commanded thee, saying, thou shalt not eat of it, cursed is the ground for thy sake, in sorrow shalt thou eat of it all the days of thy life.

All visible creation was cursed through the mixture of knowledge ingested by the first man Adam. A veil of death was cast upon all that had its base nature in earth.

Isaiah 25:7: And he will destroy in this mountain the face of the covering cast over all people, and the vail that is spread over all nations.

Since the fall of the golden age, our eyes are limited to the image man has **painted with the brush of humanistic creativity.**

There is a realm of life and activity that surrounds us that can only be envisioned by enlightened eyesight.

2 Kings 6:17: And Elisha prayed, and said LORD, I pray thee, open his eyes, that he may see. And the LORD opened the eyes of the young man; and he saw and behold the mountain was full of horses and chariots of fire round about Elisha.

Genesis 3:18: Thorns also and thistles shall it bring forth to thee; and thou shalt eat the herb of the field; in the sweat of thy face shalt thou eat bread, till thou return unto the ground; for oujt of it wast thou taken; for dust thou art and unto dust shalt thou return.

It was not by accident that Jesus wore a crown of thorns upon His head at the crucifixion

The judgment against Adam was that the earth would produce thorns and thistles. We can readily see the evidence of their presence around us as we constantly try to rid our land of their activity. God was not just declaring the natural earth would produce thorns and thistles, but this curse would also be seen within the earthy mind of man.

Read the parable of the sower in Matthew 13. This parable deals with the Word of God being sown into the earthy seed bed of Man's mind, but is choked by the **thorns and thistle growing there.**

Matthew 13:7: And some fell among thorns, and the thorns sprang up and choked the seed.

When Jesus hung on the cross, the soldiers placed a crown of thorns upon His head. There was nothing in the **mind of Christ that the thorns could identify with.** They could not choke nor destroy the word that was written within concerning who He was. He was a restored Adam, a perfect sacrifice, that would die for all mankind and become the way, the truth and the life. Our great **kinsman redeemer!**

Genesis 3:16: Unto the woman he said, I will greatly multiply thy sorrow and thy conception; in sorrow thou shalt bring forth children; and thy desire shall be to thy husband, and he will rule over thee.

God told the woman, in sorrow she would bring forth children. We read the following scripture referring to the time Jesus was born to Mary:

Luke 2:34,35: And Simeon blessed them, and said unto Mary his mother, behold, this child is set for the fall and rising again of many in Israel and for a sign which shall be spoken against, **(yea, a sword shall pierce through thy own soul also)** *that the thoughts of many hearts may be revealed.*

God was telling the woman, that even though he was promising her a seed that would restore creation, a sword would pierce through her soul. In other words she would bring forth a seed destined to die.

When Jesus hung on the cross as the last man Adam, Mary stood nearby, looking upon the promised seed of God. The word that had been made flesh within her earth, was now being crucified for the sins of the world and a **sword pierced her heart.**

Genesis 3:20: And Adam called his wife's name Eve, because she was the mother of all living.

The woman receives a name, not just a title, but a nature. Before the fall she was **woman or womb man,** Adam gave her this nature of becoming the mother of the Adam race of man, but now she would become **Eve, life giver, mother of all living.**

When Jesus died on the cross and His soul was poured out unto death. Jerusalem from above became the mother of us all. And the sons of God born from this union of Christ and His church will destroy the last enemy, death.

1 Cor. 15:26: The last enemy that shall be destroyed is death.

Genesis 3:21: Unto Adam also and to his wife did the Lord God make coats of skins, and clothed them.

We have already established the fact that Adam and Eve's nakedness was not physical, but a nakedness in the fact that they were not born of Spirit but formed from an earthy environment. The breath of God was the life that sustained them and caused them to be made a living soul.

Most of us have been taught by our religious backgrounds, that God killed an animal, took it's skin and made aprons for Adam and Eve. We were informed that this was the first blood sacrifice for man's sin.

We have already established the fact that Adam and Eve's nakedness was spiritual and not physical nudity.

There is a spiritual truth revealed here that goes beyond what we have been taught by theology.

Adam and Eve were no longer able to communicate with God in the realm of spirit because of the condemnation and consciousness of being earthy.

An animal's skin will not cover spiritual nakedness. The law of Moses had not yet been given concerning animal sacrifice, and it became necessary for God to clothe or cover Adam and Eve in order that they could continue to function in the earth as God's representative figure. He covered the spiritual body of Adam with a natural body of skin, until God Himself would visit the earth clothed in skin to redeem mankind from condemnation and death.

The Apostle Paul tells us that man has both a natural body and a spiritual body.

1 Cor. 15:44: It is sown a natural body, it is raised a spiritual body. There is a natural body, and there is a spiritual body.

Our natural body is composed of the elements found in the earth. It is an earthy house that houses our spiritual body.

Our spiritual body is eternal and was formed from the very substance of God, It is a house not made with hands.

2 Cor. 5:1: For we know that if our earthy house of this tabernacle were dissolved, we have a building of God, an house not made with hands, eternal in the heavens.

When we die our earthy house or body is buried and returns to dust. Our spiritual body however, never goes into the ground, but lives on throughout eternity. When God breathed the breath of life into the earthy man Adam, he began to be clothed in light, and the light consumed all his earthy identity. The spiritual identity of who he was shown in an outward expression so that he and his generation of Melchizedek priests became known as the great white gods.

When Jesus was transfigured on the mount of transfiguration, His spiritual body was manifested to Peter, James and John.

Matthew 17:2: And was transfigured before them, and his face did shine as the sun, and his raiment was white as the light.

His spiritual body swallowed up His earthy identity and was manifest for all to see. The true identity of who He was shone forth, body, soul and spirit.

When He died on the cross, His earthy body was laid in the tomb. Death could not hold Him and on the third day He arose as the new creation man, the first fruit of a new generation. He still carried the marks of the nail prints in His hands, but walked among mankind for forty days and nights as a witness that death nor the grave could not hold Him. His spiritual body was in complete control.

When Jesus died and rose again, He conquered death, hell, the grave, and redeemed all Adam's seed line from the affects of sin and death.

The word **redeemed** has two meanings:

1. The price paid for redemption:

1 Peter 1:18,19: Forasmuch as ye know that ye were not **redeemed with corruptible things** *as silver and gold, from your vain conversation received by tradition from your fathers; but with the* **precious blood of Christ,** *as of a lamb without blemish and without spot.*

When Jesus shed His blood on the cross as the perfect sacrifice, He died as the **last man Adam.** He paid the price for the sentence of death imposed upon man.

2. The actual deliverance of what was purchased.

Romans 8:22,23: For we know that the whole creation groaneth and travailed in pain together until now. And not only they, but ourselves also, which have the first fruits of the Spirit, *even we ourselves groan within ourselves, waiting for the adoption, to wit, the **redemption of our body.***

The **redemption of the body!** This scripture is not referring to our natural body, but speaks of the redemption of our spiritual body!

Jesus as the way, the truth and the life, revealed to us that we have a spiritual body eternal in God, that will never see death nor decay. We are waiting for the day when He actually delivers unto us the **full redemption** of what He purchased on the cross.

*2 Cor. 5:2: For in this we groan, earnestly desiring to be clothed upon with **our house which is from heaven.***

When Jesus was about to go away and leave His disciples, He began to say:

St. John 14:1,3: Let not your heart be troubled; ye believe in God, believe also in me. In my Father's house are many mansions; if it were not so, I would have told you. I go to prepare a place for you. And if I go and prepare a place for you, I will come again, and receive you unto myself, that where I am, there ye may be also.

In My Father's house are many mansions. This scripture is not referring to a geographical location we call heaven. Jesus was speaking of a **lineage.**

In the scripture, a man's family or seed line is referred to as **his house.**

Examples:

*Genesis 46:27: And the sons of Joseph, which were born him in Egypt, were two souls; all the souls of the **house of Jacob,** which came into Egypt were threescore and ten.*

*Genesis 50:8: And all the **house of Joseph** and his brethren, and his **father's house,** only their little ones and their flocks and their herds, they left in the of Goshen.*

*Exodus 16:31: And the **house of Israel** called the name thereof Manna, and it was like corlander seed, white, and the taste of it was like wafers made with honey.*

*Luke 1:27: For the time is come that judgment must begin at the **house of God;** and if it begin at us, what shall the end be of them that obey not the gospel of God?*

Galatians 6:10: As we have therefore opportunity, let us do *good unto all men, especially unto who are of the **household of faith.***

Therefore, Jesus was saying in the Father's **household of faith,** there were many mansions. Not houses made with hands , but spiritual bodies that God would indwell by His Spirit.

1 Cor. 6:19: What? Know ye not that your body is the temple of the Holy Ghost which is in you, which ye have of God, and ye are not your own?

Jesus continued to say; "I go to prepare a **place** for you."

The word place used in this scripture means: **to stay, abiding place, EXPAND TO OUTSIDE!**

Jesus was preparing the Apostles for His departure as son of man. He had become the way, the truth and the life, the divine expression of the Father unto man. He was about to leave them in the form of flesh, and was readying them for His return as the Holy Ghost ten days later.

He was relating the fact that He was going to no longer

walk among them, but would walk **in them in spirit form.** He would then **expand to the outside** of their physical bodies and bring forth the reserved portion of their inheritance, the **redemption of their body.** He had given them the example of this experience when He was transfigured before them on the mount of transfiguration.

Romans 8:11: But if the Spirit of Him that raised up Jesus from the dead dwell in you, He that raised up Christ from the dead shall also quicken your mortal bodies by His Spirit that dwelleth in you.

John 14:3: And if I go and prepare a place for you, I will come again, and receive you unto myself, that where I am, there ye may be also.

The word **receive,** used here means: **To take what is familiar from beside you into yourself.**[3]

Jesus was the eternal word clothed in flesh. He had walked as man and had become **familiar** with the human race. He was going to come again as the Holy Ghost, and **receive man** unto Himself as Spirit. This could only be possible

---

[3] Wuest

because of His familiarity with humanity.

St. John 14:16,18: And I will pray the Father, and he shall give you another comforter, that he may abide with you forever, even the Spirit of truth; whom the world cannot receive, because it seeth him not, neither knoweth him; but ye know him for he dwelleth with you, and shall be in you. I will not leave you comfortless, I will come to you.

He was coming again as the comforter, or Holy Ghost.

St. John 14:23: Jesus answered and said unto him, if a man love me, he will keep my words and my Father will love him, and we will come unto him, and make our abode with him.

The word **abode** means:

Greek 3438, Strong's: *Mone*, from Greek 3306; a staying, residence (the act or the place); abode mansion.

Chapter 6

WE ARE HIS

MANSIONS!

The Apostles had walked with Jesus for three and one-half years becoming **familiar** with His nature as Son of God. On the day of Pentecost, Jesus returned as the Holy Ghost and was received by the one hundred and twenty men and women in the upper room. They could not have **received this**

appearing, if they had not been **familiar with the man Jesus.**

Genesis 3:22: And the Lord God said, Behold, the man is become as one of us, to know good and evil, and now, lest he put forth his hand, and take also of the tree of life, and eat, and live forever.

The word **forever** means:

Hebrew 5769, Strong's: *Owlam*, From Hebrew 5956, properly concealed, the vanishing point; generally time out of mind (past or future) eternity;

Remember, the **tree of life** was also in the **midst** of Adam's garden; A **firmly established logos word,** that was the **divine expression** of God Himself.

If Adam had eaten from this knowledge, he would have lived forever concealed from sight, and vanish from the scene of God's plan and purpose of redemption.

God's plan according to *Ephesians 1:9 is: Having made known unto us the **mystery of His will,** according to His good pleasure which He hath **purposed in Himself;** That in the dispensation of the fullness of times He might gather together* *in one, all things in Christ, both which are in heaven, and which are on earth, even in Him.*

God's plan was to gather **all things into Christ, not into Adam.**

Genesis 3:24: So he drove out the man; and he placed at the east of the garden of Eden Cherubim, and a flaming sword which turned every way, to keep the way of the tree of life.

God separated Adam and Eve from the realm of light that they had walked in. They fell from a realm of Spiritual consciousness into a realm of carnality. This fall did not happen overnight, but was accomplished gradually by the flaming sword and Cherubim, placed at the **east of the garden.**

Light shines forth from the east. Adam had fallen from innocence and life into a realm of condemnation and death, because his eyes were opened to the light of God's plan and purpose to gather all things into Christ. God ordained that it would be light that would blind man's comprehension to the **true light which is Christ.**

St. Matthew 6:22: The light of the body is the eye; if therefore thine eye be single, thy whole body shall be full of light.

Adam saw light, but God would not allow his eye to be single, but drawn away to the imagination of the Cherubim.

The word Cherubim means an **imaginary figure.**

Cherubim are imaginary creatures. They represent the **imagination of man's heart.** Their images were sewn into the tapestry of the veil in the temple that separated the Holy Place from the Holy of Holies, and were seen throughout the tabernacle.

The temple Israel worshiped in was composed of three areas in it's construction; An outer court, the Holy Place, and the Holy of Holies.

These three parts represent man and his salvation. Man is body, soul and spirit. The outer court of the tabernacle represents the physical body, the Holy place our soul, and the Holy of Holies our spirit.

There is a veil of **imagery** that separates our humanity from our spirit. Imaginations are **image nations** that rule in our earth, and blind our eyes to the tree of life within.

Some of the **image nations** that rule within our earthy

temple are procrasti**nation,** indig**nation,** condem**nation,** conster**nation,** denomi**nations,** and many, many more. Our humanity is filled with graven images carved out by pioneers of past ages, who set religious boundaries founded on the Cherubim.

When Jesus died on the cross, the veil in the temple was rent from top to bottom. The way was made open, for man to boldly enter into the Holy of Holies once again and partake of the **tree of life and live forever!**

*2 Cor. 10:5: Casting down **imaginations,** and every high thing that exalteth itself against the knowledge of God and bringing into captivity **every thought** to the obedience of Christ.*

God also placed at the east of the garden, a flaming sword, which turned every way to **keep the way of the tree of life.**

We know that the word sword used in scripture represents the **word of God.**

*Ephesians 6:17: And take the helmet of salvation, and the **sword of the Spirit** , which is the **word of God.***

The sword or word that accompanied the Cherubim **turned every way** to **keep the way** of the **tree of life.**

For six-thousand years the sword has kept the way of the tree of life hidden from Adam's seed line. When man received a revelation in the word, **the sword turned.**

When the early church passed away into the **wilderness of man's interpretation,** creation sat in darkness until Martin Luther received a revelation, the just shall live by faith. What a glorious light shining in a great darkness. Because the message, **the just shall live by faith,** was a word of truth, **the sword turned.** God honored and blessed the revelation, and multitudes received the blessing of its freedom and **camped there.**

The great reformation of the church was birthed from the truth of Martin Luther's revelation, but creation was blinded to the fact it was only a small portion of truth, and not the whole.

Many revelations of the word began to be experienced by mankind, and each time the sword turned and blessed truth, a people set up camp and brought about denomi**nationa**lism. Their eyes were blinded to the fact that Jesus Christ has brought **life and immortality to light through the gospel.**

*2 Tim. 1:10: But is now made manifest by the appearing of our Saviour Jesus Christ, who hath **abolished death,** and hath brought **life and immortality to light** through the gospel.*

Jesus Christ, the **seed of the woman,** has appeared in the earth, and destroyed or rendered inactive the serpent's seed within Himself. He became the way, the truth and the life for all mankind, and **passed through the cherubim and the flaming sword for us.** He paid the price for every sin that held Adam's race under the bondage of death.

He ushered in the dispensation of grace, and through faith in His resurrection, we have life and immortality!

*1 Cor. 15:53,54: For this corruptible **must put on incorruption,** and this mortal **must put on immortality.** So when **this corruptible** shall have **put on incorruption,** and **this mortal,** shall have put on **immortality,** then shall be brought to pass the saying that is written, **death is swallowed up in victory!***

Chapter 7

CONCLUSION

Most theologians agree that there are **seven dispensations** ordained by God, to administer His will and purpose to mankind. These dispensations of time are: **innocence, conscience, human government, promise, law, grace and kingdom**.

A dispensation is a period of time, in which God dispenses His will and purpose within the **confines of its boundaries.**

The dispensations of **innocence and conscience** were during the **golden age of Adam.** In the dispensational innocence of the first man Adam, we see life manifest to all creation. When Adam and Eve's eyes were opened, the dispensation of conscience began to administer the judgment that accompanied its presence in the earth.

The dispensation of **human government** began when Noah and his sons passed through the flood, and the dispensation of **promise** was in effect during the days of Abraham.

When God visited Moses on Mount Sinai, the **law** was administered to the children of Israel, and when Jesus fulfilled the law, **grace** was bestowed upon all men.

God has always moved within the confines of a dispensation, except when an overlapping of two dispensations was in the earth.

When Jesus came to establish the dispensation of grace, He honored the law, until after He fulfilled the law through His death, burial, and resurrection.

We who are alive today find ourselves in the

overlapping of **two great dispensations.** We see the **age of grace** that has produced according to its administration, but we also see the **dispensation of kingdom** upon us. A thousand year day when Christ shall **rule in His household of faith,** bringing **all things** unto subjection to the Father.

We shall once again experience a **GOLDEN AGE!** A time when man will live and not die. A day when the kingdom's of this world become the kingdom's of our **Lord and His Christ!**

Isaiah describes this day:

*Isaiah 65:20,25: There shall be no more **an infant of days,** nor an old man that hath **not filled his days;** for the child **shall die** an **hundred years old;** but the sinner being an **hundred years old** shall be accursed. And they shall build houses and inhabit them; and they shall plant vineyards, and eat the fruit of them. They shall not build, and another inhabit; they shall not plant, and another eat; for as the **days of a tree are the days of my people,** and mine elect shall long enjoy the work of their hands. They shall not labour in vain , nor bring forth for trouble; for they are the **seed of the blessed of the Lord, and their offspring with them.** And it shall come to pass, that before they* *call, I*

Fall of the Golden Age

will answer; and while they are yet speaking, I will hear.

Life will rule in this golden age that is upon us. All creation will bask in the sunlight of the Kingdom age. What a restoration of what was lost in Adam, but found in Christ!

1 Cor. 15:55: O DEATH, where is thy sting? O GRAVE, where is thy VICTORY?

About the Author

I was born and raised in a small rural community in Southeastern Oklahoma where I attended a Nazarene Church. The church's Pastor was a woman we called "Sister Neal". Her Life was a living testimony of being wholly dedicated to God. She was such a great influence in my life that the stigma against women ministers was never an issue with me.

In 1955 my husband and I moved to Houston, Texas where I attended the Lakewood Church. My Pastor John Osteen was a powerful vessel ordained by God to be a pioneer of the Charismatic move of God in the earth. I can still hear him now declaring, "Pentecost is not a denomination, it's an experience!" On March 19th, 1959 I received this glorious baptism of fire.

In 1973, I founded the Word of Life Church and have been the Pastor for the past thirty-seven years. Through the years I have evangelized across the United States and since 2005 I have had the honor of ministering in the Philippines, India, Guatemala and Mexico. These countries continue to be a Missionary outreach for Word of Life Church.

God is so good and faithful and it has been and continues to be a wonderful journey in God. There ar*e no limits in Him and He doeth all things well.*

Made in the USA
Columbia, SC
11 August 2022

65175177R00049